Following guided prompts, this book helps you write about your life story and your most important memories.

You can draw, sketch, or add photographs to the pages to bring your story to life. Above all, enjoy completing this book.

When finished, give it back to your grandchildren so that they can go back in time and live your story.

Copyright © 2021

All rights reserved. This book or any portion thereof may not be reproduced or used in any manner whatsoever without the express written permission of the publisher except for the use of brief quotations in a book review.

Can you tell me about the time and place you were born?

What are your earliest memories?

What were you like as a child?

Do you have memories of what your parents said you were like as a baby?

Did you get into trouble as a child? What was the worst thing you did?

Describe the home you grew up in.

What was your room like? What was the best thing about it? The worst?

What were your favourite childhood toys and games?

Did you have a nickname? How did you get it?

Who was your best friend in your younger childhood years?

What do you remember about the holidays as a child?

Did you have any pets?

What was a typical day like in your family when you were little?

How would you describe a perfect day when you were young?

When you were little, what did you answer the question: "What do you want to be when you grow up?"

What did you do when you were bored as a child?

What is your best memory of childhood? Worst?

What's the most valuable thing your parents taught you?

Memories in Photos

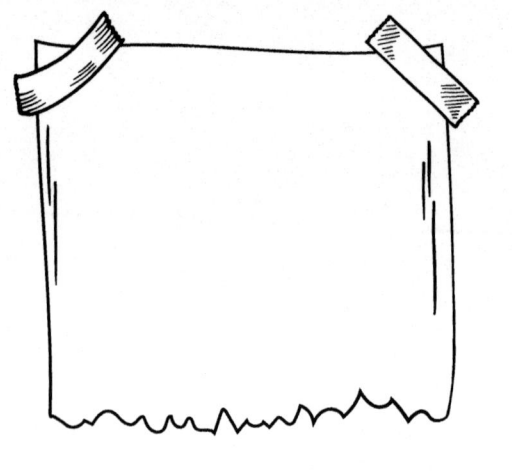

_____
_____

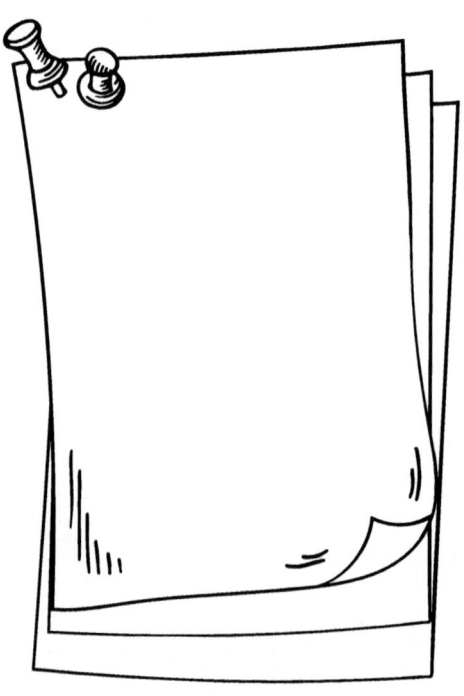

_____
_____

Memories in Photos

_____
_____

_____
_____

> *A grandfather has the wisdom of long experience and the love of an understanding heart.*

ADOLESCENCE

What were you like as a teenager?

How did you feel about school?

What type of student were you?

How would your classmates remember you?

Are you still friend with anyone from that time in your life?

What are your favourite stories from school?

What were you most embarrassed about as an adolescent? What do you think about that now?

What were you most passionate about as a teenager?

What advice would you give to your 18-year-old self?

What's the best and worst advice that you've ever been given?

Can you tell me about someone who has influenced your life? What lessons did that person teach you?

Can you tell me about one of your happiest memories of that period?

Can you tell me about one of your most difficult memories of that period?

What's your favourite: Book, Movie, Musician, Song, Quote, Animal, Word… And why?

Memories in Photos

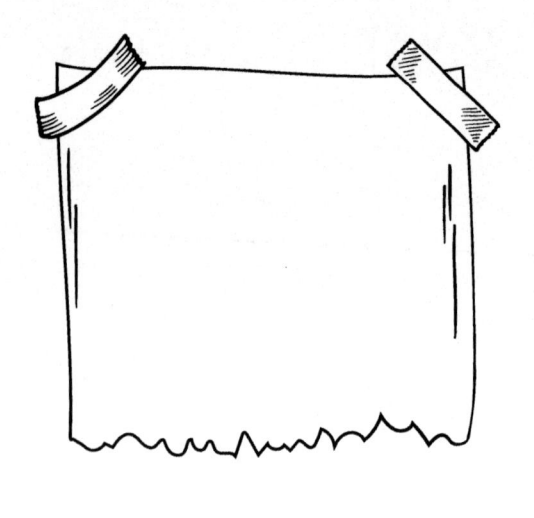

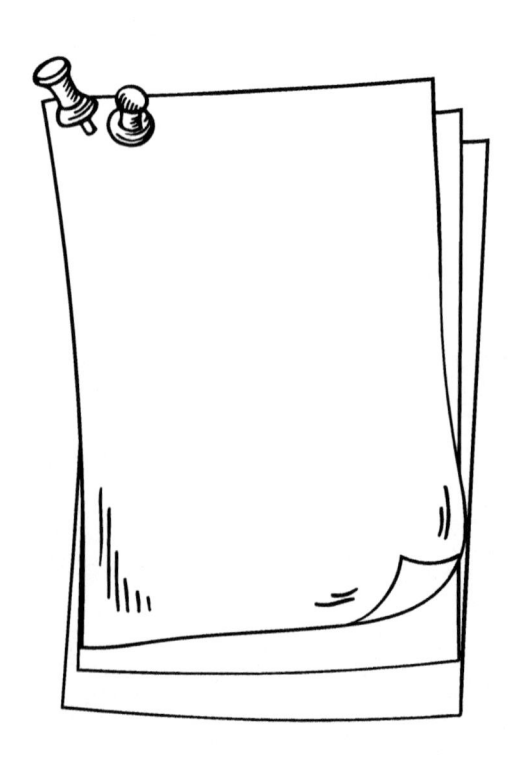

Memories in Photos

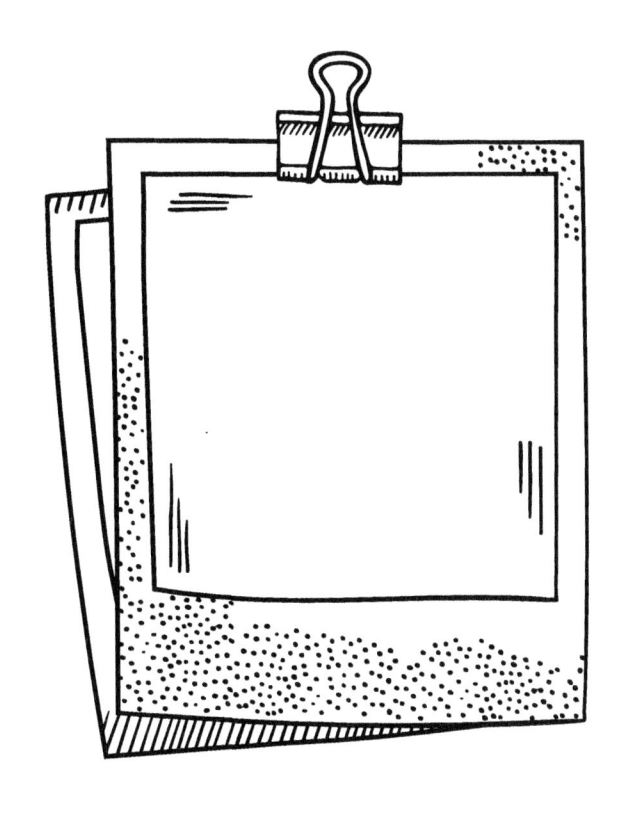

> *More and more, when I single out the person out who inspired me most, I go back to my grandfather.*

— James Earl Jones

ADULTHOOD

What was your first paying job? What did you learn from it?

Can you tell me about a memorable travel experience you had?

What do you think is the key to a successful relationship?

How did you meet grandma?

How was your wedding day?

When did you first find out that you'd be a dad? How did you feel?

Can you describe the moment when you saw your children for the first time?

How did you choose their names?

What were your children like growing up?

Do you have any favourite stories about my parent, uncles, and aunts?

What was your most memorable family vacation or trip?

What advice would you give me about raising my kids?

What is your favourite memory of me?

Are there things about me that you've always wanted to know but have never asked?

Think back to a major turning point in your life. What happened?

Do you have any regrets about your career or work life? What would you have done differently and why?

What were your proudest moments as a parent?

What do you think has stayed the same about you throughout your life? What do you think has changed?

What do you think have been the most significant inventions or technological advances in your lifetime?

What of those has specifically affected your life the most and why?

If you could have a conversation with a famous person or historical figure (alive or deceased), who would it be and what questions would you ask them?

Do you have any favourite stories from your marriage or about grandma?

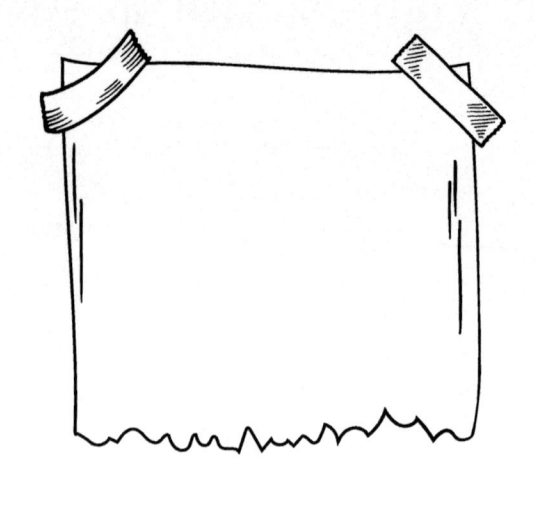

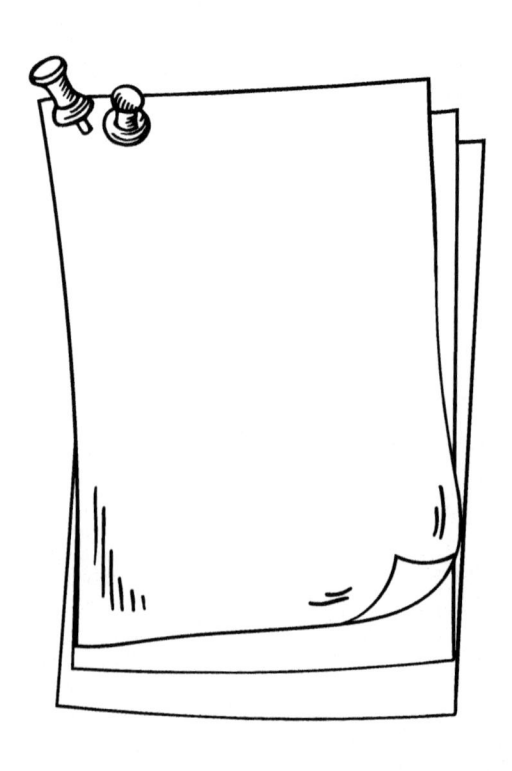

Memories in Photos

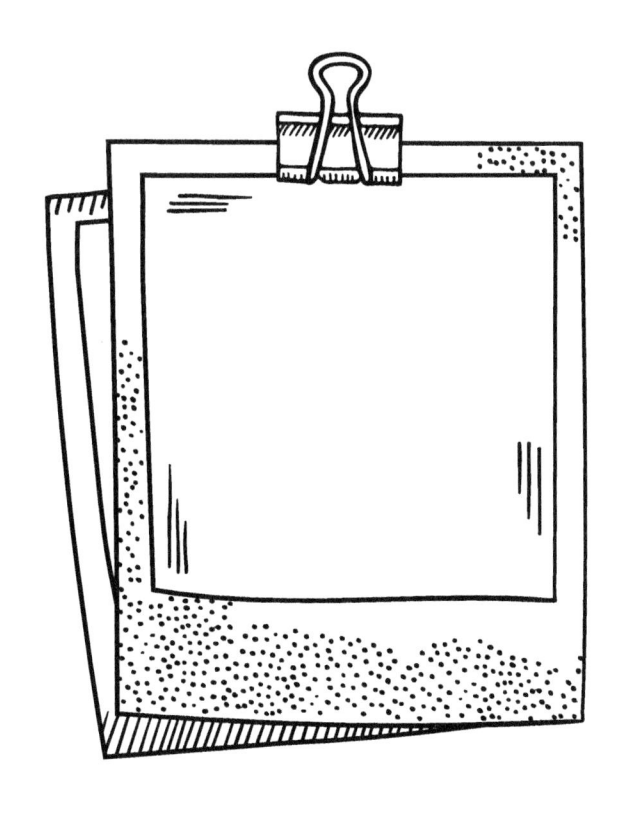

Memories in Photos

> *Grandfathers are for loving and fixing things.*

LIFE LESSONS

Can you tell me about a significant time you said "no."?

If you could go back to any age in your life, what age would that be and why?

What values would you like to pass down to the younger generations of our family?

If you could click your fingers and make one change in the world, what would it be and why?

What would you like your legacy to be?

What do you feel most grateful for in your life?

What are some of the most important lessons you've learned in life?

If you could describe your life in six words, what would they be?

_____

_____

_____

_____

_____

_____

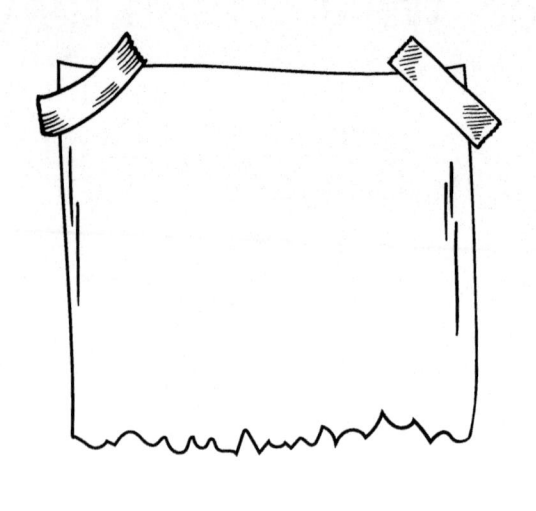

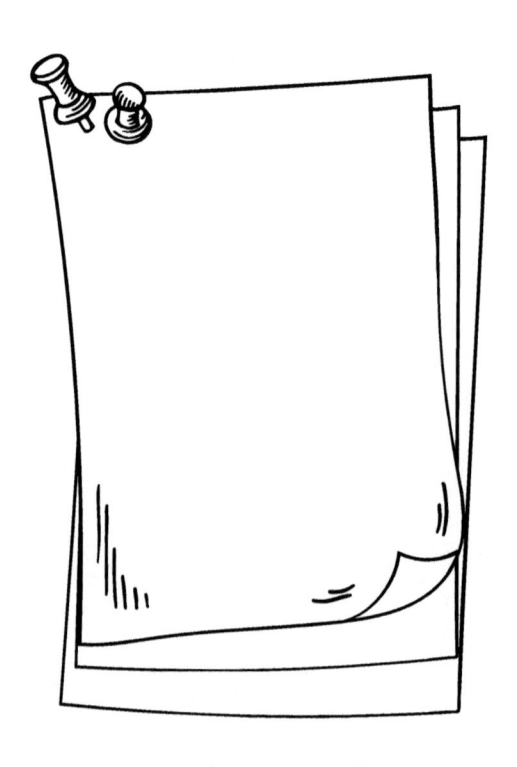

Memories in Photos

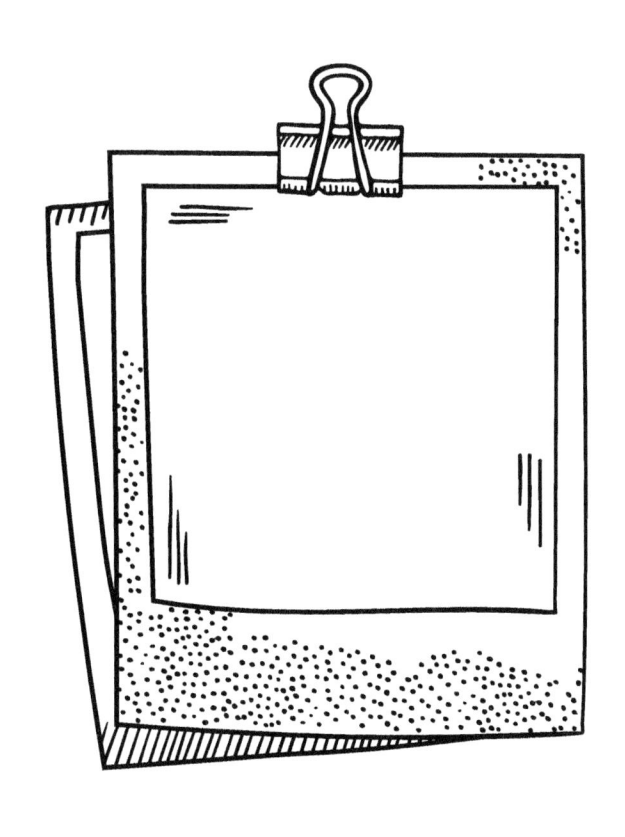

Memories in Photos

> *There is no grandfather who does not adore his grandchildren.*

— Victor Hugo

OTHER STORIES & INFORMATION

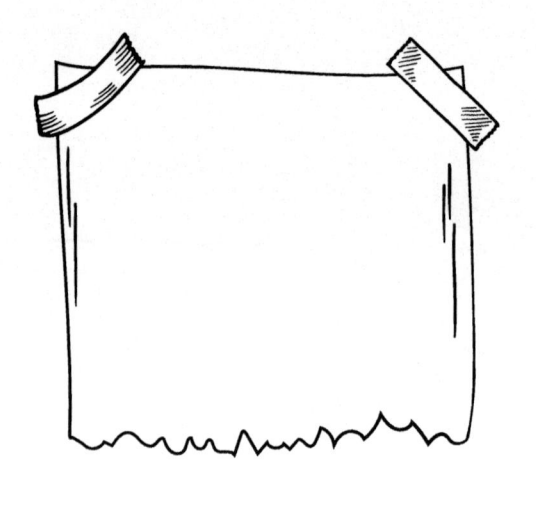

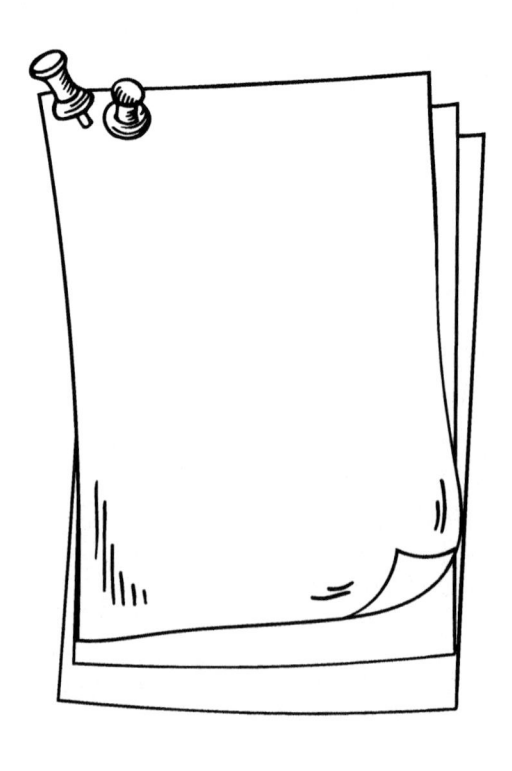

Memories in Photos

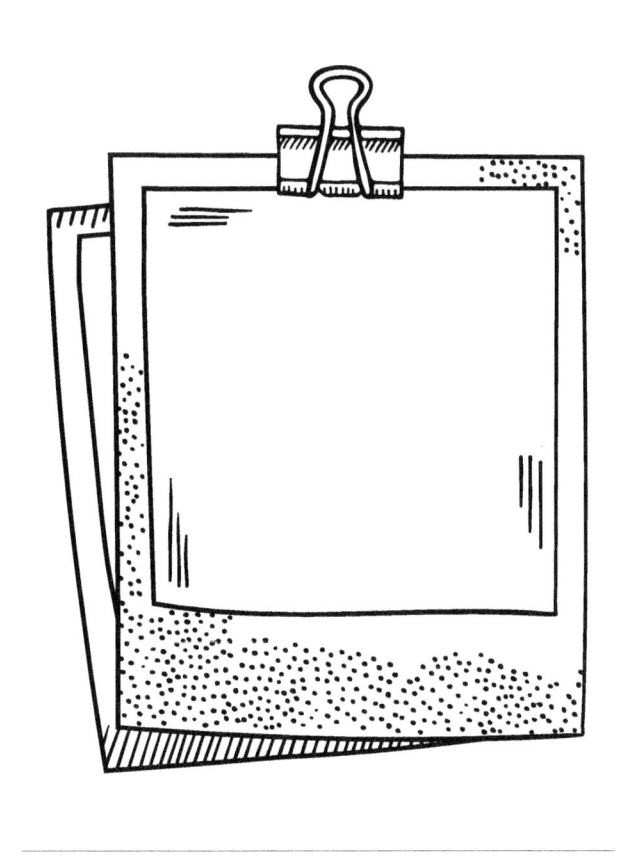

Memories in Photos

> *My grandfather did a lot of things in his life. What he was most proud of was raising his family.*
>
> – Tagg Romney

SUMMARY

CHILDHOOD

4. Can you tell me about the time and place you were born?
5. What are your earliest memories?
6. What were you like as a child?
7. Do you have memories of what your parents said you were like as a baby?
8. Did you get into trouble as a child? What was the worst thing you did?
9. Describe the home you grew up in.
10. What was your room like? What was the best thing about it? The worst?
11. What were your favourite childhood toys and games?
12. Did you have a nickname? How did you get it?
13. Who was your best friend in your younger childhood years?
14. What do you remember about the holidays as a child?
15. Did you have any pets?
16. What was a typical day like in your family when you were little?
17. How would you describe a perfect day when you were young?
18. When you were little, what did you answer the question: "What do you want to be when you grow up?"
19. What did you do when you were bored as a child?
20. What is your best memory of childhood? Worst?
21. What's the most valuable thing your parents taught you?

ADOLESCENCE

26. What were you like as a teenager?
27. How did you feel about school?
28. What type of student were you?
29. How would your classmates remember you?
30. Are you still friend with anyone from that time in your life?
31. What are your favourite stories from school?
32. What were you most embarrassed about as an adolescent? What do you think about that now?
33. What were you most passionate about as a teenager?
34. What advice would you give to your 18-year-old self?
35. What's the best and worst advice that you've ever been given?
36. Can you tell me about someone who has influenced your life? What lessons did that person teach you?
37. Can you tell me about one of your happiest memories of that period?
38. Can you tell me about one of your most difficult memories of that period?
39. What's your favourite: Book, Movie, Musician, Song, Quote, Animal, Word… And why?

ADULTHOOD

44. What was your first paying job? What did you learn from it?
45. Can you tell me about a memorable travel experience you had?
46. What do you think is the key to a successful relationship?
47. How did you meet grandma?
48. How was your wedding day?
49. When did you first find out that you'd be a dad? How did you feel?
50. Can you describe the moment when you saw your children for the first time?
51. How did you choose their names?
52. What were your children like growing up?
53. Do you have any favourite stories about my parent, uncles, and aunts?
54. What was your most memorable family vacation or trip?
55. What advice would you give me about raising my kids?
56. What is your favourite memory of me?
57. Are there things about me that you've always wanted to know but have never asked?
58. Think back to a major turning point in your life. What happened?
59. Do you have any regrets about your career or work life? What would you have done differently and why?
60. What were your proudest moments as a parent?
61. What do you think has stayed the same about you throughout your life? What do you think has changed?
62. What do you think have been the most significant inventions or technological advances in your lifetime?
63. What of those has specifically affected your life the most and why?
64. If you could have a conversation with a famous person or historical figure (alive or deceased), who would it be and what questions would you ask them?
65. Do you have any favourite stories from your marriage or about grandma?

LIFE LESSONS

70. Can you tell me about a significant time you said "no."?
71. If you could go back to any age in your life, what age would that be and why?
72. What values would you like to pass down to the younger generations of our family?
73. If you could click your fingers and make one change in the world, what would it be and why?
74. What would you like your legacy to be?
75. What do you feel most grateful for in your life?
76. What are some of the most important lessons you've learned in life?
77. If you could describe your life in six words, what would they be?

> *To a small child, the perfect granddad is unafraid of big dogs and fierce storms but absolutely terrified of the word 'boo'.*

— Robert Brault

Printed in Great Britain
by Amazon